Pres[ented to:]

My Lovely Wisa

By:

Lem

Date:

2 - 25 - 08

80 - 35 - 6

Sweet Smarts for Sweethearts

HONOR **HB** BOOKS

Inspiration and Motivation for the Season of Life

An Imprint of Cook Communications Ministries • Colorado Springs, CO

Unless otherwise indicated, all scripture quotations are taken from the *Holy Bible, New International Version* ®. NIV ®. Copyright © 1973, 1978, 1984 by International Bible Society. Used by permission of Zondervan Publishing House. All rights reserved.

Verses marked TLB are taken from *The Living Bible* © 1971. Used by permission of Tyndale House Publishing, Inc., Wheaton, Illinois 60189. All rights reserved.

Scripture quotations marked KJV are taken from the *King James Version* of the Bible.

Scripture quotations marked NASB are taken from the *New American Standard Bible*. Copyright © The Lockman Foundation 1960, 1962, 1963, 1968, 1971, 1972, 1973, 1975, 1977, 1995. Used by permission.

Scripture quotations marked NKJV are taken from *The New King James Version*. Copyright © 1979, 1980, 1982, Thomas Nelson, Inc.

Scripture quotations marked RSV are taken from the *Revised Standard Version* of the Bible, copyright © 1946, Old Testament section copyright © 1952 by the Division of Christian Education of the Churches of Christ in the United States of America and is used by permission.

08 07 06 05 04   10 9 8 7 6 5 4 3 2 1

Sweet Smarts for Sweethearts—Savvy Advice & Fun Ideas for Celebrating Love
ISBN 1-56292-180-0
Copyright © 2004 Bordon Books

Published by Honor Books
An Imprint of Cook Communications Ministries
4050 Lee Vance View
Colorado Springs, CO 80918

Compiled by Shawna McMurry.

Sweet Smarts for Sweethearts–

Savvy Advice & Fun Ideas for Celebrating Love

INTRODUCTION

Remember when you met the love of your life? Your heart raced, your mouth became dry, and your palms became sweaty. Anticipation flooded your mind with the thought of how quickly you wanted time to pass until you could be together again. Whether you are in the midst of an exciting new relationship or ready to add a new spark to an old flame, *Sweet Smarts for Sweethearts* is a fun and inspiring way to add romance to your relationship.

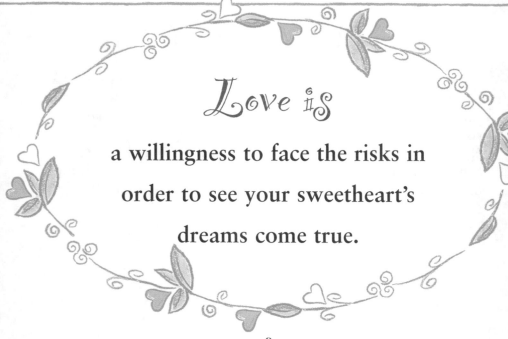

Love is

a willingness to face the risks in

order to see your sweetheart's

dreams come true.

This is how we know what love is:

Jesus Christ laid down his life for us.

And we ought to lay down our

lives for our brothers.

1 JOHN 3:16

Nathaniel came home heartbroken. How could he tell his dear wife that he had just been fired from his job at the customhouse? The last thing he wanted her to think was that he was a failure, yet he felt as if the word "failure" were embroidered across his chest. To his surprise, when he told his wife what had happened, she responded with joy. "Now you can write your book!" she exclaimed optimistically.

"And what shall we live on while I am writing it?" Nathaniel replied dejectedly.

His wife, Sophia, immediately went to a drawer and, to his amazement, pulled out a substantial sum of money and handed it to him.

"Where did you get this?" he asked, completely shocked.

"I have always known you are a man of genius," Sophia said. "I knew that someday you would write a masterpiece. Every week, out of the money you gave me for the housekeeping, I saved a little bit. Here is enough to last us for one whole year."

So Nathaniel Hawthorne, buoyed by his wife's confidence, turned his hand to writing *The Scarlet Letter.*

Love is

the active concern for the life
and growth of that which we love.

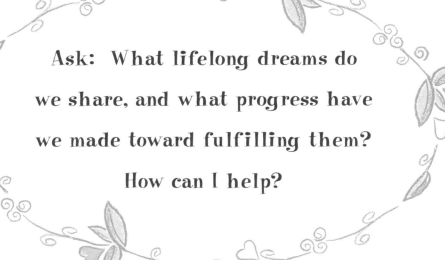

Ask: What lifelong dreams do we share, and what progress have we made toward fulfilling them? How can I help?

Romance in a Jar

Fill a jar with romance coupons for a candlelight dinner, an evening of dancing, a picnic for two, a night at the movies, or watching the sunset together. Have your sweetheart close his or her eyes and pick a "love activity" from the jar each week.

Sitting here and wanting

Not just anyone,

Desiring your every affection,

Needing no riches but instead

Candles and kisses

At a rainbow dusk.

I already love in you your beauty,
but I am only beginning to love in you that
which is eternal and ever precious—your heart,
your soul. Beauty one could get to know and
fall in love with in one hour and cease to love
it as speedily; but the soul one must learn to
know. Believe me, nothing on earth is given
without labor, even love, the most beautiful
and natural of feelings.

For what is love itself, for the one
we love best?—an enfolding of
immeasurable cares which yet are
better than any joys outside our love.

A successful marriage is a give-and-take relationship, with each party doing 90 percent giving and only 10 percent taking! Here are a few questions to ask yourself to test your ability to give and take:

1. Are you willing to give silence when your spouse needs a little quiet time?

2. Are you willing to take a rebuke and let it rest unchallenged?

3. Are you willing to give your spouse the benefit of the doubt?

4. Are you willing to take on extra chores during a time when you know your spouse is feeling stressed?

5. Are you willing to give a spontaneous word of encouragement?

6. Are you willing to take time to spend with your spouse—alone, without interruption?

7. Are you willing to give your spouse the courtesy of saying "please" and "thank you"?

8. Are you willing to take a "time out" when a disagreement appears to be overheating?

9. Are you willing to give a compliment?

10. Are you willing to take criticism?

If you couldn't answer yes to all of those questions, take heart. Marriage is a growing process. As each of you grows in your willingness to give and take, you will grow closer together.

You can keep your love alive
if you give it priority in
your system of values.

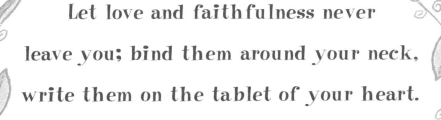

Let love and faithfulness never leave you; bind them around your neck, write them on the tablet of your heart.

PROVERBS 3:3

Talk not of wasted affection.
Affection never was wasted.

Hold hands or take your sweetheart's arm in public.

Let your sweetheart know you are proud to belong to him or her.

Make a Memory:

- Go skydiving.

- Take a hot-air balloon ride.

- Go parasailing together.

- Rent a billboard to proclaim your love for your sweetheart.

- Have a skywriter write a message for you.

- Put your love note on the marquee at a baseball stadium.

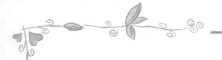

Hot Date!

Make your dinner out sizzle by adding all the extras. Bring flowers at the beginning of the date. Go one place for dinner and a better place for dessert. End the evening with a card expressing how important your sweetheart is to you.

When the Heart Is Full of Love

There is beauty in the forest
When the trees are green and fair.
There is beauty in the meadows
When wildflowers scent the air.
There is beauty in the sunlight
And the soft blue beams above.
Oh, the world is full of beauty
When the heart is full of love.

Harry and Bess

Harry S Truman first met his future bride, Bess, in Sunday school when he was six and she was just five. "She had golden curls and beautiful blue eyes," he remembered fondly. Although they graduated from high school together in 1901, the paths of their lives led in different directions until nine years later when they became reacquainted. "I thought she was the most beautiful and the sweetest person on earth," he later shared of their reunion.

From that point on, Harry began courting Bess, in part through written letters. Even after they married nine years later, the two continued their correspondence through fifty-three years of marriage, including their years in the White House. Although most of Bess's letters have been lost to history, more than thirteen hundred of Harry's missives have survived and are contained in the Truman Library collections.

How Do I Love Thee?

How do I love thee? Let me count the ways.
I love thee to the depth and breadth and height
My soul can reach, when feeling out of sight
For the ends of Being and Ideal Grace.
I love thee to the level of every day's
Most quiet need, by sun and candlelight.
I love thee freely, as men strive for Right:

I love thee purely, as they turn from Praise:
I love thee with the passion put to use
In my old griefs, and with my childhood's faith;
I love thee with a love I seemed to lose
With my lost saints—I love thee with the breath,
Smiles, tears, of all my life!—and, if God choose,
I shall but love thee better after death.

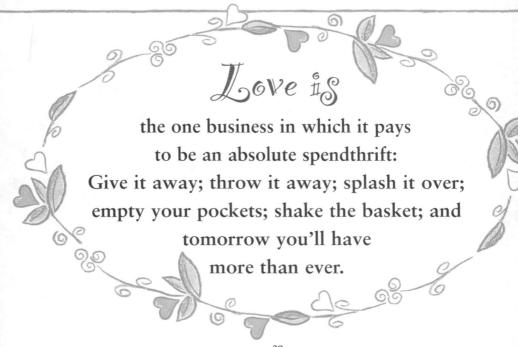

Love is

the one business in which it pays
to be an absolute spendthrift:
Give it away; throw it away; splash it over;
empty your pockets; shake the basket; and
tomorrow you'll have
more than ever.

"Give, and it will be given to you.
A good measure, pressed down,
shaken together and running over,
will be poured into your lap.
For with the measure you use,
it will be measured to you."

LUKE 6:38

Somewhere beyond the depth of your eyes
and the brilliance of your smile,
beyond the comfort of your touch,
beyond all these miles there is you.

Fountains springing from the pools
of my heart—you are their tide;
you are the unventured sea.

Reading Frost on the beach at sunrise,
all the emotions stirred
by those words are you.

Even if all becomes nothing,
there will always be you
and the memories you've given me.
This thing my heart will prove;
I can never forget you.

May you rejoice in the

wife of your youth . . .

be captivated by her love.

PROVERBS 5:18-19

Take your sweetheart out on a date which is reminiscent of your first date together. If possible, go to the same restaurant, theater, or a familiar place. Talk about memories you each have of the beginning of your romance and the feelings and thoughts you had at that time. Express to each other how your love has changed and grown over time and what feelings remain the same.

The First Day

I wish I could remember the first day,

First hour, first moment of your meeting me;

If bright or dim the season, it might be

Summer or winter for aught I can say.

So unrecorded did it slip away,

So blind was I to see and to foresee,

So dull to mark the budding of my tree

That would not blossom yet for many a May.

If only I could recollect it! Such
A day of days! I let it come and go
As traceless as a thaw of bygone snow.
It seemed to mean so little, meant so much!
If only now I could recall that touch,
First touch of hand in hand!—Did one but know.

Falling in Love

Young lovemaking, that gossamer web! Even the points it clings to—the things from which its subtle interlacings are swung—are scarcely perceptible: momentary touches of fingertips, meetings of rays from blue and dark orbs, unfinished phrases, lightest changes of cheek and lip, faintest tremors. The web itself is made of spontaneous beliefs and indefinable joys, yearnings of one life toward another, visions of completeness, indefinite trust.

There is nothing holier in this life of ours

than the first consciousness of love—

the first fluttering of its silken wings—

the first rising sound and breath of that wind

which is so soon to sweep through the soul,

to purify or to destroy.

So many marriages are rooted in passion. But to grow in depth, a marriage must be not only a "love affair," but a deep and growing friendship—a meeting not only of bodies, but of minds, hearts, and souls.

How special it is when a spouse says, "I married my best friend." Even more special is the spouse who says after many years of marriage, "I am married to my best friend!"

He is altogether lovely.

This is my beloved,

and this is my friend.

SONG OF SOLOMON 5:16 KJV

The best friend is likely to
acquire the best wife, because
a good marriage is based on
the talent for friendship.

Be kind and compassionate

to one another.

EPHESIANS 4:32

Fun Things to Do with Your Sweetheart

- Fly a kite together.
- Have a water fight.
- Climb a tree together.
- Go roller-skating.
- Make snow angels.
- Play miniature golf.
- Take a bike ride.
- Play Ping-Pong.
- Go window-shopping.

What Is Love?

To love very much is to love inadequately; we love—that is all. Love cannot be modified without being nullified. Love is a short word but it contains everything. Love means the body, the soul, the life, the entire being. We feel love as we feel the warmth of our blood, we breathe love as we breathe the air, we hold it in ourselves as we hold our thoughts.

Nothing more exists for us. Love is not a word; it is a wordless state indicated by four letters.

The Presence of Love

And in Life's noisiest hour,
There whispers still the ceaseless Love of Thee,
The heart's Self-solace and soliloquy.
You mould my Hopes, you fashion me within;
And to the leading Love—throb in the Heart

Thro' all my Being, thro' my pulses beat;
You lie in all my many thoughts, like light,
Like the fair light of dawn, or summer eve
On rippling stream, or cloud-reflecting lake.
And looking to the heaven, that bends above you,
How oft I bless the lot, that made me love you.

No small part of the zest in a good marriage comes from working through differences. Learning to zig and zag with the entanglements; studying each other's reactions under pressure; handling one another's emotions intelligently—all these offer a challenge that simply can't be beat for sheer fun and excitement.

Be quick to listen, slow to speak

and slow to become angry.

James 1:19

In the book *Rock-Solid Marriage,* Robert and Rosemary Barnes write: "Last summer we went with a close friend to his ranch in Jackson Hole, Wyoming. At our friend Gary's insistence, we spent one whole day climbing the side of a mountain to get to see something he wanted us to see. We were both just exhausted and it got to the point that we really didn't care what was in that special valley. It couldn't be worth all that pain we were going through. He just kept insisting. 'Trust me,' he kept saying, 'you'll be glad you did this when we get there.'

"Three hours later, when our feet were blistered and we were dying of thirst, we finally reached our destination. Lying down on a side of a mountain, we were looking at the most beautiful valley and lake I had ever seen. The climb was long and it was agony, but it was more than worth it. Gary was right.

"In the beginning, God established marriage. It wasn't meant to be easy; nothing worth having is. It was meant to be fulfilling and completing. It takes work. But it's almost as if God is saying, 'Trust Me, it's worth the effort!'"

Thank You, God, for teaching us to talk to one another.

Thank You for the gift of words.

Thank You for giving us each other with whom to share our hopes, our fears, our problems, and our plans.

Thank You for the assurance, that since there is no fear in love, we can be totally honest, completely ourselves, without the risk of ridicule or rejection.

Thank You for showing us the need to listen. To listen with our hearts as well as with our ears. To sense the needs that may remain unspoken beneath a torrent of words.

And to know that when there are no words to meet the situation, love can be a silent song—a touch that says,

"I'm in this situation with you," a smile that reassures, "You're doing fine."

Thank You that we have learned the need for patience; the discipline to talk things through until both minds are satisfied, even if we then return to the original solution!

Thank You for teaching a talkative partner brevity, and a quiet one how to express themselves.

Thank You, God, for teaching us to talk to one another. Thank You for the gift of words.

A couple was honored with a party on their sixtieth wedding anniversary. The husband, known for being very shy, was asked to share the secret of their long marriage. Unable to speak, he reached for a nearby fiddle and began to play.

His wife picked up the tune and began to sing.

When the song ended, the wife said simply,

"We both know all the same songs.

I never sing for any other fiddler, and

he never plays for any other singer."

When the heart is flooded with love there is no room in it for fear, doubt, or hesitation.

It is this lack of fear that makes for the dance. When each partner loves so completely that he has forgotten to ask himself whether or not he is loved in return; when he only knows he loves and is moving to its music— then, and then only, are two people able to dance perfectly in tune to the same rhythm.

You are a team.

You are not

working independently

but for one another.

Good-Night

Good-night, Good-night. Ah, good the night

That wraps thee in its silver light.

Good-night. No night is good for me

That does not hold a thought of thee.

Good-night.

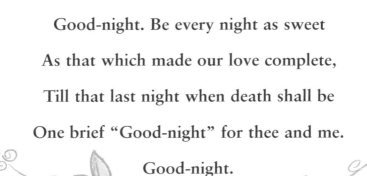

Good-night. Be every night as sweet

As that which made our love complete,

Till that last night when death shall be

One brief "Good-night" for thee and me.

Good-night.

An Old-Fashioned Date

Remember when you used to share a malt or shake with your sweetheart? Bring back those fun times by blending together two scoops of strawberry ice cream, a cup of milk, and some frozen strawberries. Pour into a tall glass and top with canned whipped cream and a cherry.

Stick in two straws, cuddle up on the sofa, and share your frosty shake. Enjoy!

Ingredients for a Romantic Evening at Home

- Scented candles
- Incense or potpourri
- Romantic music
- Favorite beverage and glasses
- Finger foods
- Romantic movie

Love Covers

Condescend to all weaknesses and
infirmities of your fellow creatures,
cover their frailties, love their excellencies,
encourage their virtues, relieve their wants,
rejoice in their friendship, overlook their unkindness,
forgive their malice, and condescend to do the lowest
offices to the lowest of mankind.

Continue to show deep love

for each other, for love makes

up for many of your faults.

1 PETER 4:8 TLB

American women expect to
find in their husbands
a perfection that English
women only hope to find
in their butlers.

Be completely humble and gentle;

be patient, bearing with

one another in love.

EPHESIANS 4:2

Be to his virtues very kind.

Be to his faults a little blind.

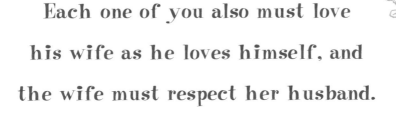

Each one of you also must love

his wife as he loves himself, and

the wife must respect her husband.

EPHESIANS 5:33

A Red, Red Rose

O my luve's like a red, red rose
That's newly sprung in June.
O my luve's like a melodie
That's sweetly play'd in tune.

As fair are thou, my bonnie lass,
So deep in luve am I;
And I will luve thee still, my Dear,
Till a' the seas gang dry.

Till a' the seas gang dry, my Dear,
And the rocks melt wi' the sun:
I will luve thee still, my Dear,
While the sands o' life shall run.

And fare thee weel my only Luve!
And fare thee weel a while!
And I will come again, my Luve,
Tho' it were ten thousand mile!

One single red rose will tell
your love she is the only
one in your life.

Each color of rose has its own meaning:

Red and white together mean unity.

Pink stands for grace and gentility.

Yellow symbolizes joy.

Orange or coral roses suggest desire.

Burgundy compliments your

sweetheart's unconscious beauty,

And white roses say, "You're heavenly!"

A Day of Roses

Fill your spouse's day with roses. Place them on the pillow, in the shower, on the kitchen table, in the car, or any other place your sweetheart goes during the course of the day.

My love was warm; for that I crossed
the mountains and the sea,
nor counted that endeavor lost
that gave my love to me.
If that indeed were love at all,
as still, my love, I trow,
by what dear name am I to call
the bond that holds me now.

Love is the most terrible,

and also the most generous

of the passions;

it is the only one that

includes in its dreams

the happiness of someone else.

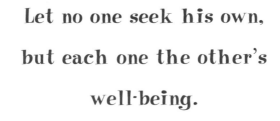

Let no one seek his own,

but each one the other's

well-being.

1 CORINTHIANS 10:24 NKJV

Washington Post columnist William Raspberry wrote a loving tribute to his wife: "The second Sunday in May was not just Mother's Day for our family—it was Mother's Graduation Day, one of the great moments in our household.

"My wife, Sondra, was one of those 'responsible' young women who decided after high school to spare her family the economic burden of college and go directly to work. Then she got married, and her family became her first priority.

"I don't know precisely what made her decide to go back to school. . . . It wasn't easy, studying part-time while managing the lives of a husband and three children. . . .

"On graduation day, it was announced that she had been inducted into both the adult honor society and Phi Beta Kappa. The kids shrieked as though she had won the Nobel prize for Smart Moms. Some people may have trouble understanding how we could get excited about something as routine as a bachelor's degree. But if you have ever taken up something difficult and made a howling success of it, you'll understand why we are so proud."

Helpful Hints for Husbands

Take half a day off work and prepare a lovely
candlelight dinner for the two of you. Surprise her
with soft, meaningful music, a bouquet of flowers,
and two tickets to see her favorite romantic film.
The next morning, serve her breakfast in bed.

. . . Or book a small hotel in the country for a
weekend break and don't tell her until you get there.
Make sure the room is stocked with fresh flowers,
candy, and scented candles.

Let me not to the marriage of true minds

Admit impediments. Love is not love

Which alters when it alteration finds,

Or bends with the remover to remove:

O no! it is an ever-fixed mark

That looks on tempests and is never shaken;

It is the star to every wandering bark,

Whose worth's unknown, although his height be taken.

Love's not Time's fool, though rosy lips and cheeks

Within his bending sickle's compass come:

Love alters not with his brief hours and weeks,

But bears it out even to the edge of doom.

If this be error and upon me proved,

I never writ, nor no man ever loved.

When I have learned to love God
better than my earthly dearest,

I shall love my earthly dearest
better than I do now.

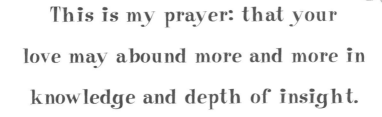

This is my prayer: that your love may abound more and more in knowledge and depth of insight.

PHILIPPIANS 1:9

Seven Daffodils

Haven't got a mansion, haven't any land

Not one paper dollar to crumple in my hand

But I can show you morning on a thousand hills

And kiss you and give you seven daffodils

Haven't got a fortune to buy you pretty things

But I can give you moonbeams for necklaces and rings

But I can show you morning on a thousand hills
And kiss you and give you seven daffodils
Seven golden daffodils shining in the sun
Light our way to evening when the day is done
And I can give you music and a crust of bread
A pillow of piney bows to rest your head.

While on vacation in New England, Sue and Kevin purchased two red "You're Special" plates at an outlet mall. They liked them so much they decided to use them as their "everyday dishes." Then one day, one of the plates broke. That night, Kevin said, "You should get the special plate tonight."

"Why?" Sue asked.

"Because you finished that big project that you were working on."

The next night, Sue insisted that Kevin dine from the "You're Special" plate, in honor of the help he had given to a neighbor in need. Thereafter, Sue and Kevin vied nightly for the "You're Special" plate honors—not to receive the plate, but to have the privilege of awarding it to the other!

When the plate finally broke, Sue said sadly, "I had never been affirmed as much in my entire life as I was these eight months that Kevin and I bestowed upon each other the 'You're Special' honors. What seemed like courtesy the first night that Kevin gave me the plate actually set a precedent for our encouraging each other on a daily basis. We're looking for another set of plates now—including one for the baby that's on the way!"

Marriage is the bond that ties two loving hearts together. As each ministers to the other, stands by the other, complements as well as compliments the other, the relationship is made fast like the strands of a rope. Love does not consist of two people gazing fondly into each other's eyes, but in moving together in the same direction.

As the maple cannot grow under the shadow of the towering oak, so one helpmate cannot develop under the domination of the other. Husband and wife, like two musicians playing different notes on different instruments, should be able to create harmony as the tones of one blend with those of the other.

The kindest and the happiest pair

will find occasion to forbear;

and something, every day they live,

to pity and perhaps forgive.

Be kind and compassionate to
one another, forgiving each other,
just as in Christ God forgave you.

EPHESIANS 4:32

Married couples who claim they
have never had an argument in
forty years either have poor memories
or a very dull life to recall.

In *Letters to Karen,* a book written to his daughter by author Charlie W. Shedd, he shares "Our Seven Official Roles for a Good, Clean Fight." They are:

1. Before we begin we must both agree that the time is right.
2. We will remember that our only aim is deeper understanding.
3. We will check our weapons often to be sure they're not deadly.
4. We will lower our voices one notch instead of raising them two.
5. We will never quarrel or reveal private matters in public.
6. We will discuss an armistice whenever either of us calls "halt."
7. When we have come to terms, we will put it away till we both agree it needs more discussing.

Be gentle and ready to forgive;

never hold grudges.

COLOSSIANS 3:13 TLB

A good marriage is that in which each appoints the other guardian of his solitude.

Romantic Suggestions

- Hold the chair for your sweetheart when she's seated for dinner.
- Open the car door for her.
- Place a flower on your wife's pillow.
- Write a love note and slip it into a book your sweetheart is reading.
- Take a quiet walk together while holding hands.
- Write your sweetheart's name in the snow.
- Make time for a pillow fight.

- Write a special message on the bathroom mirror using lipstick, soap, or shaving cream.

- Buy an antique key and give it to your loved one inside a card; tell your sweetheart it's the key to your heart.

- Take a hot-air balloon ride together.

- Snuggle up and take turns reading a book out loud together.

Love Is Eternal

Inside the wedding band that Abraham Lincoln gave Mary Todd were engraved the words, "Love is eternal." As Lincoln lay dying in a rooming house across the street from Ford's Theatre, where he had been the victim of an assassin's bullet, Mary Todd Lincoln twisted the gold band on her left hand. Had any other marriage ever undergone the strain of theirs? The war . . . the loss of a son . . . Mary's irrational behavior . . . and now this.

When the President breathed his last, someone in the room declared, "He belongs to the ages." Mary's response was, "He belongs to me. Our love is eternal."

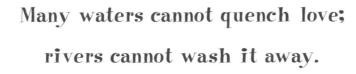

Many waters cannot quench love;

rivers cannot wash it away.

SONG OF SOLOMON 8:7

To My Dear Loving Husband

If ever two were one then surely we.

If ever man were loved by wife, then thee;

If ever wife were happy in a man,

Compare with me, ye women, if you can.

I prize thy love more than whole mines of gold

Or all the riches that the East cloth hold.

My love is such that rivers cannot quench,

Nor aught but love from thee give recompense.

Thy love is such I can no way repay,

The heavens reward thee manifold, I pray.

Then while we live, in love let's so persevere

That when we live no more, we may live ever.

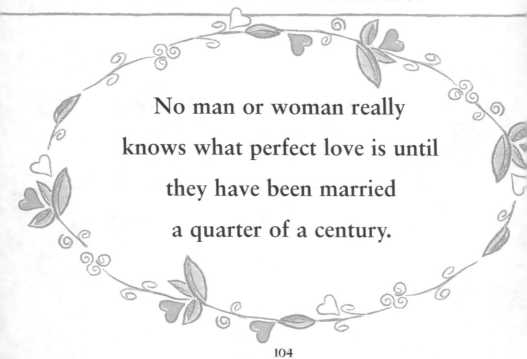

No man or woman really
knows what perfect love is until
they have been married
a quarter of a century.

Grow old along with me!

The best is yet to be,

The last of life, for which the first was made:

Our times are in His hand

Who saith, "A whole I planned,

Youth shows but half; trust God: see all,

Nor be afraid!"

A Faithful Love

In *A Time for Remembering,* Ruth Bell Graham writes that when she was a teenager, leaving her childhood home in China for schooling in Korea, she fully intended to be an old maid missionary to Tibet. She did, however, give some thought to the particulars she would require in a man if she could ever be persuaded to marry. She wrote in her diary: "If I marry: He must be so tall that when he is on his knees, as one has said, he reaches all the way to heaven. His shoulders must be broad enough to bear the burden of a family.

His lips must be strong enough to smile, firm enough to say no, and tender enough to kiss. Love must be so deep that it takes its stand in Christ and so wide that it takes the whole lost world in. He must be active enough to save souls. He must be big enough to be gentle and great enough to be thoughtful. His arms must be strong enough to carry a little child."

Did Ruth Bell find such a man in Billy Graham? Perhaps not on the day she met him as much as on the day they celebrated their fiftieth wedding anniversary.

The success of a marriage comes
not in finding the "right" person,
but in the ability of both partners
to adjust to the real person they
inevitably realize they married.

Pillow talk between partners

can soften a rocky pilgrimage.

Mike Mason, author of *The Mystery of Marriage,* writes: "[Marriage] is an alliance of love, and love is a spiritual vehicle, a rocket ship, that travels faster and farther than anything else under the sun.

"Get out of it for a moment, and it leaves without you for parts unknown; let it idle, and it begins to rust; neglect it, and it seizes right up.

"It can be a full-time job just being a passenger in this thing. But like it or not, you and your spouse are in it together, and the work of traveling in marriage is the most vital work you can do. In the Lord's plans for the world there is no work more important than the work of relationship, and no relationship is more important than that of one's marriage."

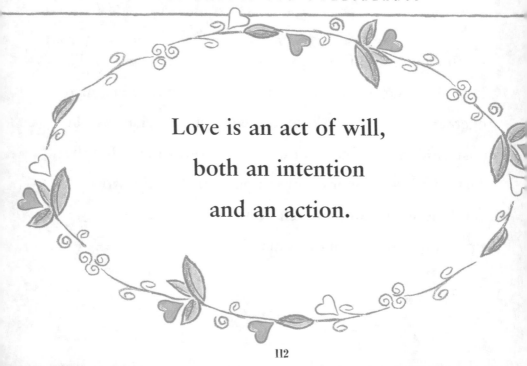

Love is an act of will,

both an intention

and an action.

Let us not love with words

or tongue but with actions

and in truth.

1 JOHN 3:18

Don't think that love, to be true,
has to be extraordinary.
What is necessary is to continue to love.
How does a lamp burn,
if it is not by the continuous
feeding of little drops of oil?
When there is no oil, there is no
light and the bridegroom will say:
"I do not know you."
Dear friends, what are our drops of oil in our lamps?

They are the small things from everyday life: the joy,
the generosity, the little good things,
the humility and the patience.
A simple thought for someone else.
Our way to be silent, to listen, to forgive,
to speak and to act . . . are the real drops of oil
that make our lamps burn vividly our whole life.
Don't look for Jesus far away, He is not there.
He is in you; take care of your lamp
and you will see Him.

A teacher once asked her group of kindergartners to answer the question, "What is love?" One little girl piped up, "Love is when your mommy reads you a bedtime story." Another little girl quickly added, "And real love is when she doesn't skip any pages."

Every person needs to feel that they are truly acknowledged and made to feel important. But we also need to know this need for recognition is received in different ways. What one person may receive as an expression of approval and appreciation may not be received in the same way by another person.

Find out what is meaningful to your spouse. For some, an expression of importance may be the amount of time spent with your spouse or special care given to details. In other cases, your spouse may experience great encouragement from words of praise

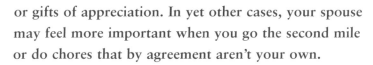

or gifts of appreciation. In yet other cases, your spouse may feel more important when you go the second mile or do chores that by agreement aren't your own.

Notice things that make your spouse feel special; then make a mental note of it and purpose to do it for them again. Become a student of your spouse's heart.

"My command is this:

Love each other

as I have loved you."

JOHN 15:12

Gift Ideas

Give your loved one a gift that will symbolize your love for each other now and in the future. Start a plant in a special place that will grow with your love. Or, get a gift you can share, such as matching jewelry, complementary clothing, or membership to a club or organization.

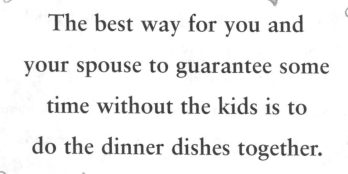

The best way for you and
your spouse to guarantee some
time without the kids is to
do the dinner dishes together.

Groaning as he helped his wife wash the dishes one evening, the Reverend John Byrnell protested, "This isn't a man's job!"

His wife immediately wiped her hands and reached for the family Bible on the nearby dining table. "Oh, yes it is," she said as she turned to 2 Kings 21:13 KJV and read aloud to her husband, "I will wipe Jerusalem as a man wipeth a dish, wiping it, and turning it upside down."

Doing things together is the essence of a healthy marriage.

Sharing the housework

makes it easier to

share the love.

Bear one another's burdens,

and so fulfil the law of Christ.

GALATIANS 6:2 RSV

Let him kiss me with the kisses

of his mouth—for your love is

more delightful than wine.

Pleasing is the fragrance of your perfumes;

your name is like perfume poured out.

Song of Solomon 1:2-3

Four sweet lips, two pure souls,
and one undying affection—
these are love's pretty
ingredients for a kiss.

The most wonderful of all things in life, I believe, is the discovery of another human being with whom one's relationship has a glowing depth, beauty, and joy as the years increase. This inner progressiveness of love between two human beings is a most marvelous thing; it cannot be found by looking for it or by passionately wishing for it. It is a sort of Divine accident.

I lie beside you and sometimes it seems
That every day is just living a dream.
We've grown together through passing years.
We've shared our secrets and our fears.
We've seen the sun rise. We've seen the sun fall.
I know that you know I gave you my all.
I've held you when you've laughed.
You've held me when I've cried.
So I promise to always stay in love
With that magical light in your eyes.

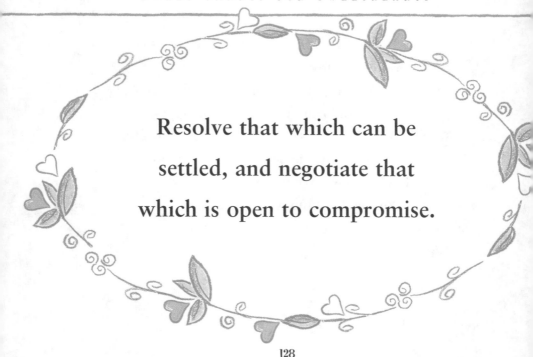

Resolve that which can be settled, and negotiate that which is open to compromise.

[Love] is not self-seeking.

1 CORINTHIANS 13:5

Pamela, from Europe, met her husband, Steve, while they were both traveling in Israel. After a romantic, whirlwind courtship, they married. Within three years, Pam found herself living in a small town in the United States, caring for two babies. The hardest part of the transition in her life, however, was the change she saw in Steve. He worked long hours, stayed out late with friends, and did little to help her with the children.

A counselor helped Pam take a look at her own life. She soon recognized that there was a difference in her own behavior in their getting-along times and their times of conflict. In a nutshell, when Pam was nice to Steve, he was nice to her. With this new awareness, Pam set about to change her ways. When Steve came home late, she didn't protest. She simply asked how his day had gone. Before too many days, Pam noticed that Steve was coming home earlier. Then one Saturday, he got up early to take care of the children so she could sleep in. She was thrilled.

If you feel that things have changed, it might be good to ask yourself, *Am I different?*

Ideas for a Romantic Date with Your Spouse

- Go on a moonlight picnic. Don't forget the blanket and a book of poetry.

- Sleep out under the stars, just the two of you.

- Take a walk together under the light of a full moon.

- Go dancing together.

- Kidnap your spouse for a prearranged overnight excursion to a local bed-and-breakfast.

- Make arrangements to go horseback riding.

Ideas for a
Romantic Evening at Home

- Watch the sunset together.
- Picnic on your fire escape or patio, or in the backyard.
- Spread a blanket on the living room floor and have an indoor picnic.
- Read old cards and letters from each other to each other.
- Enjoy pizza by candlelight.
- Stay up all night eating popcorn and watching old movies.

A man found a wallet in the street one day. There was no identification inside—only three dollars and a crumpled letter with a barely legible return address on the envelope. When he opened the letter, he discovered it had been written some sixty years ago by a woman named Hannah. She was explaining to a man named Michael that her mother wouldn't allow her to see him again, but that she would always love him.

The man set out to find Hannah. He soon located her in a nursing home.

She was seventy-six and had never married—there had just never been anyone like Michael. As the man was leaving, the doorman noticed the wallet and said, "That's Mr. Goldstein's. He's one of the old-timers on the eighth floor." The man immediately went to see Mr. Goldstein, now seventy-eight, who told him he had never married—no one had been like Hannah. The man said, "I think I know where she is," and he escorted Michael down to the third floor where he was reunited with his beloved!

Three weeks later, Michael and Hannah married, a perfect ending to a genuine love.

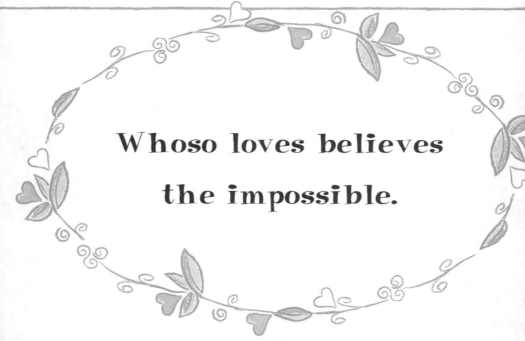

Whoso loves believes the impossible.

Love cannot be forced;

Love cannot be coaxed and teased.

It comes out of Heaven,

Unasked and unsought.

You have a lifetime to

enjoy one another.

Don't waste a day of it.

Live happily with the woman
you love through the
fleeting days of your life.

ECCLESIASTES 9:9 TLB

Love Is Forever

On the day after Jack Benny's death in December 1974, a single long-stemmed red rose was delivered to Mary Livingstone Benny, his wife of forty-eight years. When the blossoms continued to arrive, day after day, Mary called the florist to find out who sent them. "Quite a while before Jack passed away," the florist told her, "he stopped in to send a bouquet.

"As he was leaving, he suddenly turned back and said, 'If

anything should happen to me, I want you to send Mary a single rose every day.'" There was complete silence on Mary's end of the line. Then weeping, she said, "Good-bye."

Subsequently, Mary learned that Jack had actually included a provision for the flowers in his will, one perfect red rose daily for the rest of her life.

What greater thing is there for two human souls

than to feel that they are joined for life—

to strengthen each other in all labor,

to rest on each other in all sorrow,

to minister to each other in all pain,

to be one with each other

in silent, unspeakable memories

at the moment of the last parting.

Love Coupons

Make a love coupon that you print yourself and leave on your spouse's pillow. Here are a few suggestions:

- Breakfast in bed
- Dinner for two
- An evening stroll
- One big bear hug

Advice to Her Son on Marriage

When you gain her Affection, take care to preserve it;
Lest others persuade her, you do not deserve it.
Still study to heighten the Joys of her Life;
Not treat her the worse, for her being your Wife.
If in Judgement she errs, set her right, without Pride:
'Tis the Province of insolent Fools, to deride.

A Husband's first Praise, is a Friend and Protector.
Then change not these Titles, for Tyrant and Hector.

Let your Person be neat, unaffectedly clean.
Tho' alone with your wife the whole Day you remain.
Chuse Books, for her study, to fashion her Mind,
To emulate those who excell'd of her Kind.
Be Religion the principal Care of your life,
As you hope to be blest in your Children and Wife:
So you, in your Marriage, shall gain its true End;
And find, in your Wife, a Companion and Friend.

Love Song

There is a strong wall about me to protect me:
It is built of the words you have said to me.
There are swords about me to keep me safe:
They are the kisses of your lips.
Before me goes a shield to guard me from harm:
It is the shadow of your arms between me and danger.
All the wishes of my mind know your name,

And the white desires of my heart
They are acquainted with you.
The cry of my body for completeness,
That is a cry to you.
My blood beats out your name to me,
Unceasing, pitiless
Your name, your name.

To love is to find pleasure

in the happiness of

the person loved.

Serve one another in love.

GALATIANS 5:13

To Husband and Wife

Preserve sacredly the privacies of your own house, your married state, and your heart. Let no father or mother or sister or brother ever presume to come between you or share the joys or sorrows that belong to you two alone.

With mutual help build your quiet world, not allowing your dearest earthly friend to be the confidant of aught that concerns your domestic peace. Let moments of

alienation, if they occur, be healed at once. Never, no never, speak of it outside; but to each other confess and all will come out right. Never let the morrow's sun still find you at variance. Renew and renew your vow. It will do you good; and thereby your minds will grow together contented in that love which is stronger than death, and you will be truly one.

When you go on a business trip, make it a point to send a note of appreciation and love. Pre-mail cards so that your spouse will receive a special message each day that you are gone, or send e-mail cards to let your sweetheart know you're thinking about him or her.

Love cannot remain by itself—it has no meaning. Love has to be put into action and that action is service. Whatever form we are, able or disabled, rich or poor, it is not how much we do, but how much love we put in the doing; a lifelong sharing of love with others.

Do not merely look out for your own personal interests, but also for the interests of others.

PHILIPPIANS 2:4 NASB

Love Refines

Love refines

The thoughts, and heart enlarges, hath his seat

In reason, and is judicious, is the scale

By which to heavenly love thou mayest ascend.

Lord, make us instruments of Thy peace.

Where there is hate, may we bring love;

Where offense, may we bring pardon;

May we bring union in place of discord;

Truth, replacing error;

Faith, where once there was doubt;

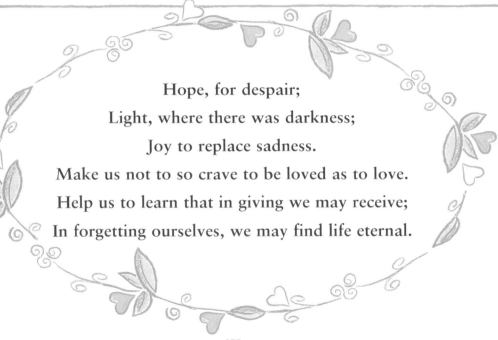

Hope, for despair;

Light, where there was darkness;

Joy to replace sadness.

Make us not to so crave to be loved as to love.

Help us to learn that in giving we may receive;

In forgetting ourselves, we may find life eternal.

Acknowledgments

Erich Fromm (12), William H. McMurry III (15, 34, 35), Count Lev
Tolstoy (16), George Eliot (17, 40, 142), Dr. James Dobson (20, 128, 138),
Henry Wadsworth Longfellow (22, 41), Thomas C. Haliburton (27),
Elizabeth Barrett Browning (30, 31, 136), Christina Rossetti (38, 39),
Friedrich Nietzsche (44), Guy de Maupassant (47), Samuel Taylor
Coleridge (48, 49), Charlie W. Shedd (50), Marion Stroud (54, 55), Anne
Morrow Lindberg (58), Janette Oke (59), S. Weir Mitchell (60, 61),
William Law (64), W. Somerset Maugham (66), Robert Burns (70-71),
Robert Louis Stevenson (75), Jean Baptiste Alphonse Karr (76), William
Shakespeare (83), C.S. Lewis (84), Traditional American (86-87), Paul
McElroy (90, 91), William Cowper (92), Rainer Maria Rilke (97), Anne
Bradstreet (102-103), Mark Twain (104), Robert Browning (105), John
Fisher (108), Muriel James (109), M. Scott Peck (112), Mother Teresa
(114, 115, 152), Sir Hugh Walpole (126), Pearl S. Buck (137), Mary Barber
(144-145), Mary Carolyn Davies (146, 147), Leibnitz (148), John Milton
(153), Antoine de Saint-Exupery (155), St Frances of Assisi (156, 157).

Additional copies of this book and other titles by Honor Books
are available from your local bookstore.

If you have enjoyed this book, or if it has impacted your life,
we would like to hear from you.
Please contact us at:
Honor Books
4050 Lee Vance View
Colorado Springs, CO 80918
www.cookministries.com